NORTH-EAST ENGLAND FROM ABOVE

CONTENTS

INTRODUCTION

THE FOUR COUNTIES THAT FORM THE NORTH-EAST OF ENGLAND — Cleveland, Tyne and Wear, Durham and Northumberland — stretch from the northern county limits of Yorkshire all the way up to the Scottish border. Here is a region of extremes: cities and towns of modern industry, lowland farming, remote hills indented by dales, and high moors. To the west the region is bounded by the Pennines and to the east by a long coastline fringing the North Sea, with scattered islands and lighthouses. Lindisfarne, or Holy Island, is the cradle of early Christianity in England.

Newcastle-upon-Tyne is the regional capital with its famous bridges, including the first large-scale cast-iron bridge ever built. Newcastle and neighbouring Wallsend mark the end of Hadrian's Wall. Durham is a beautiful city situated on the river Wear, its famous Norman cathedral and castle standing on a high sandstone bluff almost surrounded by a natural moat formed by a loop in the river.

The county of Durham is a mature landscape of fields with hedgerows and higher up a network of drystone walls. There are frequent villages, market towns and coalfields. Further south are the heavier industrial areas of the Tyne and Tees estuaries in Tyne and Wear and Cleveland. To the north, lies the vastness of Northumberland.

In Roman times, Northumberland was a wild frontier land, protected against Scottish invasion by soldiers guarding Hadrian's extraordinary wall, parts of which are extremely well preserved. In the centuries that followed Roman occupation, many towns changed ownership several times during bloody battles between the Scots and the English. The raiding and pillaging officially came to an end in 1707 with the Act of Union between England and Scotland, although peace did not happen overnight. While the rich and powerful lived in fortified castles, lesser folk built thick-walled *pele* towers on to their properties or sought refuge elsewhere if attacked. In 1541, at least 120 castles existed — a testimony to the insecurity in the region. Not until the 18th century was Northumberland transformed into peaceful agricultural use, with enclosures and roads. Even today this frontierland holds a sparse population and a sense of quiet remoteness pervades the landscape.

Photographs from top to bottom: Otterburn, Gateshead Millennium Bridge, Corstopitum Roman Fort, Blyth

PHOTOGRAPHS, TEXT AND DESIGN BY ADRIAN WARREN AND DAE SASITORN

MYRIAD BOOKS LIMITED

FARNE ISLANDS (ABOVE)

THE **F**ARNE **I**SLANDS CONSIST OF **28** ISLANDS, situated between 3-8km off the coast near Bamburgh. Formed from volcanic rock, the islands have a distinctive black appearance. Nowhere in the British Isles can such a variety of sea birds, including 50,000 pairs of puffins, be found in such a small area. Another resident of the islands is the grey seal, the largest carnivore in the British Isles. The 4,000-strong colony here is one of the most important in Europe.

LINDISFARNE (LEFT AND RIGHT)

LINDISFARNE OR **H**OLY **I**SLAND, on the coast between Berwick and Bamburgh, is a key site in the history of Christianity in Britain. In AD635 St Aidan founded a monastery built of wood that was to become the spiritual and educational heart of Northumbria. It flourished under St Cuthbert until repeated attacks by the Vikings forced the monks to flee in terror in 875. After the Norman Conquest, Benedictine monks from Durham renamed Lindisfarne "Holy Island" to commemorate the holy blood shed during the Viking invasions. The monks built a **PRIORY** (right) in stone that remained until Henry VIII's Dissolution in 1536. Then it was abandoned and its stone plundered to build **LINDISFARNE CASTLE** (left) to defend the island against possible Scots incursions. A garrison remained at the castle until the late 19th century. Twice each day the tide sweeps across the causeway, severing the link with the mainland for several hours.

BERWICK-UPON-TWEED (ABOVE)

BERWICK-UPON-TWEED, the most northerly town in England, has changed hands between England and Scotland no less than 13 times as a result of the struggle for the Anglo-Scottish frontier. In the 14th century King Edward I fortified it against Scottish attack. Some of the town walls, dating mainly from the Elizabethan period and the finest of their kind in Europe, can still be seen. The "Old Bridge" across the river Tweed was built in 1611 from red sandstone and has 14 arches.

DUNSTANBURGH CASTLE
(ABOVE)

DUNSTANBURGH CASTLE, sited on a crag above the sea, was built early in the 14th century for Thomas Earl of Lancaster, nephew of King Edward II. Later, Thomas had many disagreements with the King and was executed in 1322. In 1362, John of Gaunt, fourth son of Edward III, inherited the castle. It was a Lancastrian stronghold during the Wars of the Roses (1455-1485) and suffered heavy damage from cannon, leaving the castle in ruins.

CRASTER (LEFT)

JUST 2.5KM SOUTH OF DUNSTANBURGH CASTLE is the village of Craster, internationally famous for its traditionally oak-smoked kippers and salmon. About a mile from the village is Craster Tower, dating from the 15th century, the home of the Craster family, who have been here since before the Norman conquest. Craster has prospered from the local stone that was shipped off to London to become kerb stones.

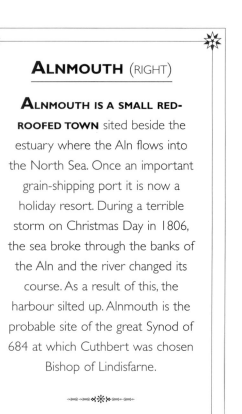

ALNMOUTH (RIGHT)

ALNMOUTH IS A SMALL RED-ROOFED TOWN sited beside the estuary where the Aln flows into the North Sea. Once an important grain-shipping port it is now a holiday resort. During a terrible storm on Christmas Day in 1806, the sea broke through the banks of the Aln and the river changed its course. As a result of this, the harbour silted up. Alnmouth is the probable site of the great Synod of 684 at which Cuthbert was chosen Bishop of Lindisfarne.

⟶⟶⟶ ❊ ⟵⟵⟵

HULNE PRIORY (LEFT)

THE RUIN OF HULNE PRIORY, situated to the northwest of Alnwick is the site of the first Carmelite monastery in Britain. It was founded in 1240 and was even fortified. The 4th Earl of Northumberland, Henry de Percy, built a tower in 1488 to protect the monks during border troubles with the Scots. The surviving remains include the tower and a defensive precinct wall. The chapel has been transformed into a residence. The site was used as Maid Marion's garden in Kevin Costner's film *Robin Hood: Prince of Thieves*.

WARKWORTH CASTLE (ABOVE)

WARKWORTH CASTLE IS SITUATED overlooking the River Coquet. The original motte and bailey castle was built in the 12th century but is famously associated with the Percy family of Alnwick Castle (see page 8), who acquired it in 1332. The Percy's power struggles brought them into frequent conflict with the monarchy, and a failed uprising of the Northern Earls against Queen Elizabeth led to the execution of the 7th earl in 1572, and to the pillaging of the castle, which subsequently fell into gradual decay.

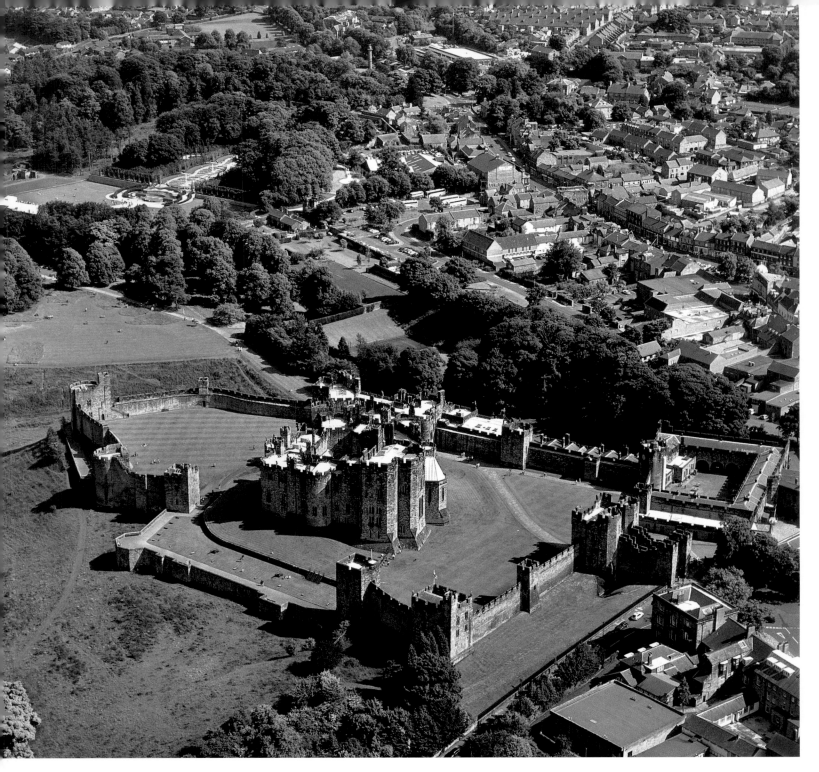

ALNWICK CASTLE (LEFT)

ONE OF THE FINEST MEDIEVAL CASTLES in England, Alnwick is home to the Duke of Northumberland and has been the seat of the Percy family since 1309. It is the second largest inhabited castle in the country. The castle was originally built by the Norman baron, Yvo de Vescy, in 1096, but was considerably altered over time by the Percy family.

WHITLEY BAY (RIGHT)

WHITLEY BAY IS A PRETTY SEASIDE RESORT which was highly fashionable around the start of Queen Victoria's reign and prospered when a railway connection to Newcastle was built. Along with Cullercoats and Tynemouth, Whitley Bay is one of Newcastle's nearest seaside resorts.

BLYTH (RIGHT)

THE BLYTH HARBOUR WIND FARM was built in 1992, the UK's first semi-offshore farm with nine machines set along the harbour wall. There are also two offshore wind turbines: the first in UK waters and the largest erected offshore anywhere in the world (see photograph on contents page). The history of the port dates back to the 12th century. It reached its peak as a coal shipping port in the 1960s. The shipbuilding yard was the largest on the north-east coast until it closed in 1967.

KIELDER WATER (LEFT)

CLOSE TO THE SCOTTISH BORDER AND HADRIAN'S WALL, Kielder Water is
the largest man-made lake in Europe. The lake sits within the massive Kielder
Forest, Britain's largest, home to red squirrels, deer and many rare birds.
Predominantly a planted forest of sitka and Norway spruce, it is currently
being replanted to include a wider range of species including many
broadleaved trees. Fossil evidence shows that a tropical forest once grew here.

NORTHUMBERLAND NATIONAL PARK (ABOVE)

NORTHUMBERLAND NATIONAL PARK stretches from the Scottish border
south to Hadrian's Wall covering an area of more than 1,030 sq km
(400 sq miles). The upland scenery of the Cheviot Hills dominates the north
of the national park, with wide open moorland rising to 815m (2,674ft).
Further south, there are pastures and river valleys. The remains of
medieval castles litter the landscape.

HADRIAN'S WALL
(ALSO SEE BACK COVER)

IN AD121, THE ROMAN EMPEROR HADRIAN decided to build a wall across the neck of England in order to guard the constantly threatened north-west frontier. The wall stretches for 117km (73 miles) from the mouth of the River Tyne in the east to the Solway Firth in the west, following the crest of ridges which added to the impregnability of his barrier. Manned by up to 12,000 men, there were 16 forts along its length.

HOUSESTEADS FORT (left) is close to the halfway point along the wall, just inside Northumberland.

At **CHESTERS FORT** (above right), to the north of Hexham, Hadrian's Wall crossed the North Tyne river by means of a bridge. The site is famous for the foundations of a Roman bath house, one of the best preserved in Britain. Hadrian's Wall is without doubt the most important monument left by the Romans in Britain, invoking a dramatic image of a country divided by conflict and occupation.

CORSTOPITUM (BELOW RIGHT)

JUST WEST OF THE VILLAGE OF CORBRIDGE is the site of Corstopitum, a Roman fort built around AD80 by the Roman Governor of Britain Julius Agricola. Not part of Hadrian's Wall, it guarded an important crossing of the River Tyne, and the junction of two important Roman roads. It also played a strategic role in the attempted conquest of Caledonia. After Hadrian's Wall was built, it became a military supply base. A large settlement of tradesmen and merchants grew around it so that it became one of the most important Roman towns in the wall country.

POPPY FIELD NEAR CORBRIDGE (LEFT)

A FIELD OF POPPIES, *Papaver rhoeas*, near Corbridge sets the landscape ablaze with colour. Corbridge, in Northumberland, literally grew from the Roman town of Corstopitum which provided the building stones for many of the village buildings, including the church, and nearby castles. In the 13th century Corbridge was second only to Newcastle in wealth. Its bridge became derelict by the 17th century, and was finally replaced in 1674.

HEXHAM (RIGHT)

HEXHAM IS THE LARGEST TOWN in Tynedale. In Anglo-Saxon times, an abbey was founded here by Saint Wilfrid, who was educated on the holy island of Lindisfarne. Hexham was regarded as one of the finest towns in the country and was built using stones taken from the ruins of Hadrian's Wall and the Roman fort at Corbridge. In 875, Hexham and its abbey were damaged by the Vikings and were repeatedly a target for Scottish raids.

ASHINGTON (LEFT)

ASHINGTON LIES ON THE NORTH bank of the River Wansbeck. The history of this area is dominated by the coal-mining industry. By the late 19th century Ashington had grown into a large colliery village, expanding even further in the early 20th century into "the largest mining village in the world". Ashington, like most other local mines, was shut down in the late 20th century. There are now no deep mines left in the entire region.

OTTERBURN (PREVIOUS PAGE)

IN 1388, THE ENGLISH AND SCOTTISH armies faced each other at the battle of Otterburn. Despite the loss of their leader, the Scots routed the English and thousands were killed. The site of the battle is marked by Percy's Cross, a stone column just outside the village. For centuries here in Northumberland, families on both sides of the border raided each other's lands, stole cattle and burned crops in violent blood-feuds.

NEWCASTLE-UPON-TYNE (BELOW AND RIGHT)

THE REGION'S CAPITAL IS PERCHED ON the northern banks of the river Tyne. Among the mixture of buildings old and new are the Cathedral of St Nicholas and the castle keep, built in 1172, bounded by the quayside and the famous bridges linking the city with Gateshead. Newcastle began as a minor fort on Hadrian's Wall which starts nearby at Wallsend. A city wall built in 1280 protected Newcastle from attacks by Scottish raids. The city prospered as a result of coal, and during the industrial revolution grew as a centre for heavy engineering and shipbuilding. Below left is the High Level Bridge for road and rail, built in 1849 and designed by the railway engineer George Stephenson. Armstrong's Swing Bridge sits in the middle. It was built in 1876 on the site of a former medieval bridge. To the right is the familiar arch of the famous Tyne Bridge. When it was constructed in 1928, it was the largest single span bridge in the world.

GATESHEAD MILLENNIUM BRIDGE (ABOVE)

GATESHEAD IS NEWCASTLE'S "TWIN TOWN", lying on the opposite bank of
the Tyne — and there is great rivalry between the two places . It is an industrial
centre situated in a former coal-mining region. First settled in Roman times, it
grew in importance under the Saxons. The Gateshead Millennium Bridge is the
first opening bridge to be built across the River Tyne for more than 100 years
and has a unique design. It provides a footpath and cycleway linking new arts
and cultural developments at Gateshead Quays with Newcastle, including the
Baltic centre for contemporary art, and the Sage centre for music.

SUNDERLAND (ABOVE)

SITUATED AT THE MOUTH OF THE RIVER WEAR, Sunderland was a centre for shipbuilding and a port for the export of coal as long ago as the 14th century. Glass-making and potteries began during the 17th and 18th centuries when the industrial revolution and the railway brought growth and prosperity. Today, with a population of 300,000, Sunderland is the largest town in the north-east.

A1(M) NEAR WASHINGTON (LEFT)

THE NEW TOWN OF WASHINGTON is divided into 16 districts, some built on the sites of old villages. Washington Old Hall was the home of the ancestors of George Washington, the first president of the United States. The connection dates from 1180 when William de Hartburn bought the manor and changed his name to William de Washington, the first member of the family which gave its name to the capital city of the USA.

21

TYNEMOUTH PRIORY AND CASTLE (ABOVE)

TYNEMOUTH'S HEADLAND commands the northern approaches to the River Tyne and has been a strategic defence against threats from medieval Scotland, 19th-century France and 20th-century Germany. Founded in 1090 on the site of an ancient Anglian monastery, it has been a burial place for saints and kings. The history of Tynemouth Castle is closely connected with that of the Priory, both of which stand on the same rocky headland.

RABY CASTLE (RIGHT)

RABY CASTLE WAS A LARGE FORTIFIED MANSION house that has been developed into an impressive stately home. John, 3rd Baron Nevill, obtained a licence to construct a castle in 1378 and it evolved over many generations into the great fortress it is today. Visitors can admire the greatest medieval kitchen in England (virtually unchanged since the 14th century) and Raby Castle's famous walled gardens.

DURHAM (LEFT)

THE CENTRE PIECE OF THE UNIVERSITY CITY OF DURHAM is sited on a dramatic sandstone bluff almost surrounded by a steep banked wooded bend in the river Wear. Dominating this natural fortress are the castle and the Norman cathedral, one of the finest in Europe. The castle was built in 1609 to guard the "neck" of the peninsula formed by the meandering river. The cathedral was founded as a shrine for the body of St Cuthbert, brought here by the monks of Lindisfarne, fleeing from Viking raids.

LUMLEY CASTLE (RIGHT)

SITUATED 1.5KM EAST OF CHESTER-LE-STREET, Lumley Castle dominates the countryside across the River Wear. It was built in 1392 as a manor house and was later converted by Sir Ralph Lumley, whose descendants include "Lily of Lumley", a ghost who reputedly haunts the castle. It remained for centuries the seat of the Lumley family. Today, Lumley castle is a hotel and restaurant where popular "Elizabethan Banquets" are held.

FINCHALE PRIORY
(LEFT)

JUST TO THE NORTH-EAST OF DURHAM by a bend in the river Wear, are the ruins of Finchale — pronounced "finkle" — Priory. It was the home of a 12th-century hermit, St Godric, who built a small chapel here dedicated to St John as a result of a vision. The Hermit lived here until his death aged 105. Later the monks at Durham took over the site and it was transformed during the 13th century into a priory.

SEAHAM (ABOVE)

SEAHAM — OR SEAHAM HARBOUR — as it is better known, developed as a result of the coal-mining industry. Once the dock was established in the 1850s, Seaham became a centre for moving coal from local pits to London by ship. New quays, large curving piers and a lighthouse were constructed in the early 20th century to give the harbour the unusual shape we can see today. It was at Seaham Hall on the northern outskirts of the town that the poet Lord Byron married Anne Isabella Milbank, daughter of a wealthy local family.

BOWES MUSEUM (RIGHT)

THE IMPOSING CHÂTEAU of the Bowes Museum is situated near Barnard Castle in County Durham. It was founded in 1892 by John and Josephine Bowes and designed by the French architect Jules Pellechet. Alongside the extensive permanent collections of paintings, ceramics, antique furniture and textiles, the museum holds exhibitions and concerts.

BARNARD CASTLE (ABOVE)

BARNARD CASTLE, perched high on rocky cliffs overlooking the River Tees, gives its name to the surrounding beautiful, historic market town. The castle was originally built from timber but rebuilt in stone by Bernard de Balliol in the 12th century.

In 1569, during the "Rising of the North", 5,000 rebels supporting Mary Queen of Scots besieged the castle after which it fell into ruin. In 1630 it was sold to Sir Henry Vane who used it as a source of materials for improvements to Raby Castle.

GUISBOROUGH (RIGHT)

THE MARKET TOWN OF GUISBOROUGH lies just outside the Tees valley south of Middlesbrough. Originally, it was the capital of Cleveland and is certainly one of the most historic towns in the area. The ruins of Guisborough's beautiful Augustinian priory and its surrounding gardens dominate the town. The priory was founded in 1119 by Robert De Brus.

MIDDLESBROUGH (LEFT)

MIDDLESBROUGH DEVELOPED AS THE LARGEST port on the Tees thanks to its deep water harbour and the extension of the Stockton and Darlington railway in the 1830s carrying coal from the nearby coalfields. In 1850 iron ore was discovered nearby. Iron replaced coal as the lifeblood of the town and by 1900 Middlesbrough's population had grown to 90,000. The great explorer James Cook was born at Marton, a suburb of Middlesbrough in 1728.

RIVER TEES NEAR TEESMOUTH (RIGHT)

IN THE 17TH AND 18TH CENTURIES commerce and industry on the River Tees was still in its early stages, but in the Victorian age it boomed. Today, Teesside is the site of one of the largest petrochemical industries in Europe and is also a leading producer of iron and steel. The deep-water ports of Tees handle millions of tonnes of shipping cargo each year.

HARTLEPOOL
(RIGHT)

A MONASTERY WAS FOUNDED HERE in Saxon times in about 640 and a fishing village grew up beside it. The monastery was destroyed by the Danes in the 9th century but the village of Hartlepool grew. Hartlepool was transformed in the 1830s when the railway was built to the town making it possible to export coal from the Durham coalfield. At this time the shipbuilding, iron and steel industries boomed.

LAST REFUGE Ltd

Nature is a precious inheritance, to be cared for and cherished by all of us. Last Refuge Ltd is a small company primarily dedicated to documenting and archiving endangered environments and species in our rapidly changing world, through films, images and research. The company was established in 1992 for a study of wild giant pandas in the Qinling mountains of central China, which seemed, literally, to be the "last refuge" for these charismatic animals. The company continued to embrace new projects worldwide. Two films on lemurs in Madagascar quickly followed and the ring-tailed lemur became the company's logo. Adrian Warren and Dae Sasitorn, who run the company from a farmhouse in Somerset, have created a special website, www.lastrefuge.co.uk, in order to present their work. This is becoming a huge resource for information, and an extensive photographic archive of still and moving images for both education and media. Ultimately they hope to offer special conservation awards to fund work by others.

ADRIAN WARREN

Adrian Warren is a biologist and a commercial pilot, with over 30 years' experience as a photographer and filmmaker. He has worked worldwide for the BBC Natural History Unit, and as a director in the IMAX giant screen format. He has recently designed a new wing-mounted camera system for aircraft to further develop his interest in aviation, aerial filming and photography. As a stills photographer, he has a personal photographic archive of over 100,000 pictures, with worldwide coverage of wildlife, landscapes, aerials, and peoples. His photographs appear in books, magazines, advertisements, posters, calendars, greetings cards and many other products. His awards include a Winston Churchill Fellowship; the Cherry Kearton Medal from the Royal Geographical Society in London; the Genesis award from the Ark Trust for Conservation; an International Prime Time Emmy; and the Golden Eagle Award from New York.

DAE SASITORN

Dae Sasitorn is an academic from the world of chemistry but has given it up to follow her love for the natural world. She manages the company and is a computer expert. She has created, designed and manages the Last Refuge website as well as scanning thousands of images for the archive. She is also a first-class photographer in her own right.

THE PHOTOGRAPHY

Adrian and Dae operate their own Cessna 182G out of a tiny farm strip close to their house. They bought the single engined four-seater aircraft in May 1999 in order to develop a new wing-mounted camera system for cinematography. The 1964 Cessna was in beautiful condition, and had only one previous owner. It is the perfect aircraft for aerial work: small, manoeuvrable, with plenty of power, and the high wing configuration offering an almost unrestricted view on the world below. With 20 degrees of flap it is possible to fly as slowly as 60 knots. The cabin side window opens upwards and outwards and is kept open by the airflow. Over London, however, where it is not permitted to fly a single engine fixed wing aircraft in case of engine failure, the Cessna had to be abandoned in favour of a helicopter. The photographs were taken on Hasselblad medium format 6 x 6 cm cameras and lenses using Fujichrome Velvia film. Waiting for the right weather, with a clear atmosphere and less than 50 per cent cloud cover, required being on standby for months.

First Published in 2004 by Myriad Books Limited,
35 Bishopsthorpe Road, London, SE26

Photographs and Text ©
Dae Sasitorn and Adrian Warren
Last Refuge Limited

ISBN 1 904154 86 7

Designed by Dae Sasitorn and Adrian Warren
Last Refuge Limited
Printed in China